Kid's Library of Space Exploration

Traveling to the Moon

Space Exploration

Kid's Library of Space Exploration

Traveling to the Moon

Kim Etingoff

Kid's Library of Space Exploration: Traveling to the Moon

Village Earth Press
Vestal, New York 13850
www.villageearthpress.com

First Printing
9 8 7 6 5 4 3 2 1

Series ISBN (paperback): 978-1-62524-444-4
ISBN (paperback): 978-1-62524-404-8
ebook ISBN: 978-1-62524-039-2

Library of Congress Control Number: 2014931524

Author: Etingoff, Kim.

Contents

ONE

Early History

No one had to discover our moon. You look up, and it's there! But for a long time, no one knew much about the moon. What was it made of? How far away was it? Why did it change shape?

Today we can answer all those questions. Not only have we answered those questions and more, we've also flown to the moon. Twelve men have actually walked right on its surface.

Flying to the moon and back has been one of humankind's greatest achievements. Governments, astronauts, scientists, and engineers had to work hard to get people to the moon. Now we have a better understanding of the moon than ever before.

Moon Magic, Moon Science

The moon has always fascinated people. Ancient peoples had many ideas about it. Some thought it might be a ball of fire or a mirror. The Romans, for example, believed the moon was a goddess called Luna.

The word "lunar," which refers to the moon, comes from the name of the Roman goddess. In China, people called the moon goddess Chang'e.

Some people believed (and still do today) that the moon has to do with how people act. The thought was that a full moon made people crazy. The word "lunatic" refers to people going crazy because of the moon. Teachers today sometimes swear that their students are wilder during the full moon!

And don't forget werewolves! People were said to have changed into werewolves when the moon was full.

Whether or not the moon influences people's behavior, it does have an affect on Earth's oceans. The tides change as the moon moves around the Earth. When the moon is over a certain part of Earth, its gravity pulls on the ocean a little, causing a high tide in that part of the world. When the moon moves on around the Earth, its gravity pulls in a different direction, causing a low tide.

The moon also affects the *climate* on this planet. It may affect other things on Earth, too, such as the way the Earth's crust moves. Scientists still don't know everything about the moon.

The first time people could get a closer look at the moon was when telescopes were invented. In 1609 Galileo, an Italian astronomer, was the first person to use a telescope to look at the night sky. Among other things, Galileo looked at the moon with his telescope. He saw a rough surface with craters and mountains. Before, people had thought the moon was smooth.

Other astronomers looked at the moon, too. They mapped out the part of the moon we can see. They even gave every feature a name.

To the Moon

By the twentieth century, people knew a lot more about the moon. Astronomers had figured out the "holes" in the moon were caused by things crashing into it. They had started to figure out the history of the moon.

But people were still studying the moon from Earth. We couldn't get any closer. At least not yet.

Climate is the overall kind of weather in a particular region or on a particular planet.

Eventually, we started to build technology that would allow us to study the moon from space. People were really interested in space exploration by the 1950s. Governments put a lot of money toward it. Many scientists worked on studying space.

Two governments in particular were really involved with space exploration. One was the United States. The other was the Soviet Union, which is now Russia and several other countries.

The United States and the Soviet Union were competing with each other after the end of World War II. Each one wanted to be the most powerful country in the world. They never really fought directly in a war, but there was a lot of tension between them.

Part of that competition had to do with space. The two countries were rushing to be the best at space exploration. They were in a space race. At first, the Soviets were ahead. They sent the first man-made *satellite* into space in 1957. It was called *Sputnik 1*. The Americans weren't far behind, though. They sent up a satellite in 1958.

The Soviets were the first to launch a person into space, too. *Cosmonaut* Yuri Gagarin went up in a Vostok spacecraft in 1961. He circled around Earth and safely came back down.

The United States wasn't going to let the Soviets win. The government set up the National Aeronautics and Space Administration (NASA) to win the space race. NASA was going to get to the moon before the Soviet Union.

The government gave NASA a lot of money. Many scientists and engineers worked for NASA. The 1950s and '60s were a busy time for NASA.

A *satellite* is something that travels around something else in space.

Cosmonauts are the same as astronauts, except they participate in the Russian space program instead of NASA.

Moon Phases

The moon isn't actually changing shape when it goes from new moon to full moon and back again. The sun lights up only half of the moon. That's the side we can see. As the moon circles around Earth, we can only see part of the lit-up side. When we see just a sliver, we call it a crescent moon. When we can see half the lit-up side, it's a half-moon. And when we see the whole side, it's a full moon.

This was the first picture of both the Earth and its moon within the same frame. It was taken by the probe Voyager 1 as it sped away from the Earth. Today, Voyager 1 is still operational, though it has left our solar system.

Lunar Orbiters

Before anyone could send a person to the moon, we had to figure out how to fly a spacecraft to the moon. NASA and Rocosmos, the Soviet space administration, set to work.

The Soviet Union was the first to send a spacecraft to the moon. *Luna 1* was a spacecraft that was meant to fly to the moon and then crash into it. The Soviet Union launched *Luna 1* in 1959. However, it missed the moon, flying by it.

The next spacecraft was called *Luna 2*. This time, the Soviets were successful. *Luna 2* crashed into the moon and took some measurements.

More Luna spacecraft were sent up. Some made it, and some didn't. Several were meant to land softly on the surface but either didn't make it to the moon or crashed into it instead.

There were also some successful soft landings, too. *Luna 9* was the first spacecraft to land softly on the moon. It took pictures and measured radiation levels.

Luna 10 was the first spacecraft to enter orbit around the moon. In 1966 it made it to the moon and started circling around it. More *Lunas* followed later.

Meanwhile, the United States came up with the Lunar Orbiter program. It would build spacecraft to fly to the moon and then circle it. They would be practice for sending humans to the moon.

Each cone-shaped orbiter had two cameras onboard to take photos. The photos showed the best places for people to land. They also gave scientists a better idea of what the moon was like.

President Kennedy and the Moon

The president of the United States at the beginning of the space race was John F. Kennedy. He famously urged the United States to do everything it could to send someone to the moon. In 1961 he gave a speech about going to the moon. He told Americans and the world, "We choose to go to the moon in this decade and do the other things, not because they are easy, but because they are hard, because that goal will serve to organize and measure the best of our energies and skills, because that challenge is one that we are willing to accept, one we are unwilling to postpone, and one which we intend to win, and the others, too." Within ten years, the United States lived up to President Kennedy's speech and sent humans to the moon.

An image of the moon's surface taken by one of the Apollo 10 *astronauts. The Apollo program allowed humans a closer look at the moon than we'd ever had before.*

The orbiters could also gather information about the moon's environment. They could find out how much radiation from the sun there was. They could measure how much gravity the moon had. All those measurements were needed to make the moon safe for humans.

The Lunar Orbiter program started in 1964. *Lunar Orbiter 1* launched two years later. For thirty-five days, the orbiter traveled to and around the moon. The very first orbiter was a success! Four more Lunar Orbiters successfully made it to the moon.

All together, the orbiters photographed almost the whole surface of the moon. The five orbiters took 1,654 high-quality photographs. Scientists picked out good landing sites from the pictures. They would use those sites for future missions carrying people.

Next Steps

Both the Soviet Union and the United States were getting closer to landing a person on the moon. But they still had a little more work to do before that could happen.

The Soviets tried out several Zond missions. Like the Luna missions, no one was on board. Computers and other machines ran the missions.

The Zond missions tested out spacecraft that could fly to the moon and back to Earth. The sun powered these spacecraft. Several Zond missions successfully came back to Earth. However, they also had problems. If anyone had been onboard, they would have been killed. That's why the Soviet Union was only doing tests!

Zond 5 was the first spacecraft to go to the moon and return to Earth. *Zond 5* carried several kinds of living things to test the effects of space on life. Aboard were turtles, worms, flies, seeds, plants, bacteria, and more.

Scientists opened the spacecraft after they retrieved it from its landing in the ocean. The living things all survived. The Soviets had proven living things could fly around the moon and safely return home. Maybe humans could too.

The Soviet Union had made a lot of progress toward sending people to the moon. The United States thought the Soviet Union might beat them to the moon.

The crew of the failed Apollo 1 *mission. From left to right: Edward White, Gus Grissom, and Roger Chaffee.*

But the United States was working on its own missions. After the earlier Gemini program, NASA created the Apollo program. The goal of the Apollo program was to eventually land humans on the moon and bring them back home.

The Apollo program started out with unmanned missions. Like the Zond missions, they were meant to test out spacecraft that could fly to the moon and back. The first manned Apollo mission was *Apollo 1*. Unfortunately, the program started out with a disaster.

Apollo 1 was set to launch in February 1967. NASA had picked three astronauts to be the first men to fly by the moon. They were command pilot Gus Grissom, senior pilot Edward White, and pilot Roger Chaffee.

The *Apollo 1* spacecraft was pretty complex, and this was the most complicated mission NASA had ever flown. The spacecraft had some construction problems, which engineers tried to fix.

Less than a month before launch, NASA did a launch *simulation*. This was a test to see if the launch would actually work. But the spacecraft didn't actually lift off.

The three astronauts were inside *Apollo 1* during the test. They had their space suits on. They were ready to go.

After some problems, the countdown began. Suddenly, a fire started. It spread quickly and then the spacecraft broke open. The astronauts couldn't get out, and all three died. The whole thing took only a few seconds.

Apollo 1 was a tragedy, but NASA didn't end the program there. After an investigation into the accident, NASA spent a long time fixing problems and redesigning the spacecraft. Then they were ready to keep going all the way to the moon.

Big Money

Space programs cost a lot of money. In the middle of the twentieth century, the US government spent a lot of money on sending people to the moon. The Apollo program cost NASA over $19 billion. And that was only a third of what NASA spent overall during the same time period!

A *simulation* is when you perform a test to see if something will actually work.

Find Out Even More

Reading books about the things that you find interesting is one of the best ways to learn more. But a book can only hold so much information about a subject. One book can't tell you everything about a topic or idea. The author of the book had to choose what to leave out. To get more information—to get a better view of a subject—you'll almost always have to read more than one book. With so many books to read about so many things, you can always learn more.

To find other books about the subjects you love, check out your school or local library. At the library, discovering new books is as easy as asking the librarian. You can also search the library's card catalog for books of all sorts. The books listed below might be a good list to get started with if you're looking for other books about missions to the moon. If the library near you doesn't have these books, you should be able to find many other books about astronauts, rockets, and space.

Chaikin, Andrew. *Mission Control, This Is Apollo: The Story of the First Voyages to the Moon*. New York: Viking Juvenile, 2009.

Edwards, Roberta. *Who Was Neil Armstrong?* New York: Grosset & Dunlap, 2008.

Floca, Brian. *Moonshot: The Flight of Apollo 11*. New York: Atheneum/ Richard Jackson Books, 2009.

Thimmesh, Catherine. *Team Moon: How 400,000 People Landed Apollo 11 on the Moon.* New York: HoughtonMifflin, 2006.

Take a look at the pages of the books you find in the library. In the front of the book, you'll probably see the table of contents. Find a chapter that stands out to you and flip to that page. Read over a few of the pages. Flip through other pages in the book and look at the index or glossary. Ask yourself a few questions after looking at the book.

1. How well do you understand the book? Every book isn't made for every reader. Finding a book that's written in a way you really understand is a big part of becoming a better reader. Don't forget to challenge yourself, but make sure the book you're reading works for you.
2. How is the book organized? How do the table of contents and index help you find information in the book? Try using the table of contents or index to find something in the book you find exciting or interesting.
3. Is there information in this book that you haven't read in another? Are there any facts that you have read in other books?
4. Are there photos or pictures in the book? Do they help you to better understand information about the subject in the book? Are there captions (words under the pictures)? How do they add to the book? Seeing what you're picturing in your head as you read can be a great way to learn more about many subjects.

TWO

Apollo 11

NASA used several space missions to practice for the moon. First up were several unmanned Apollo missions. These were followed by manned missions.

Manned Missions

After testing out spacecraft, NASA planned for the first manned mission to the moon. No one would land on the moon yet. But they would fly all the way there and come back safely. Even that was a big step forward for space exploration.

The first manned mission was *Apollo 7*. Astronauts Donn Eisele, Walt Cunningham, and Wally Schirra were onboard. The point of *Apollo 7* was to test the spacecraft to make sure everything worked perfectly for later moon missions.

The Saturn V rocket was used to launch all of the Apollo missions.

The crew successfully made it into space. They circled around Earth 163 times. The whole mission lasted eleven days. There was a live TV camera on-board, too. People on Earth watched the first live TV pictures from space.

Even the return journey was perfect. The astronauts splashed down in the ocean and were picked up and returned home.

Apollo 8 tried something new. This time, the crew was launched into space and put into orbit around the moon. The three astronauts on the crew saw the far side of the moon. No other human had ever seen it in person.

Apollo 9 and *10* were more *manned* test flights. Each one showed that NASA could safely send people to the moon in the spacecraft they had designed.

Landings

Each Apollo spacecraft was meant only to be used once. As it reentered Earth's atmosphere, the command module separated from the rest of the spacecraft. Inside were the astronauts. The command module safely fell into the ocean, while the rest burned up. Then the astronauts were picked up by boat and returned home.

Finally

Finally, NASA was ready to launch a moon landing. If all went according to plan, humans would set foot on the moon.

Something that is ***manned*** is piloted by humans instead of controlled from far away.

The space race was still going on. So far, the Soviet Union had beaten the United States in a lot of things. But now it looked like the United States could still win the race—if it could land a person on the moon first.

The space race-winning mission was called *Apollo 11*. It was launched in July 1969. As usual, three astronauts were chosen as the crew. They were commander Neil Armstrong, command module pilot Michael Collins, and lunar module pilot Buzz Aldrin. All three had flown into space before.

The crew of the Apollo 11 *mission. Commander Neil Armstrong, seen here on the left, would become famous for his role as the first human to walk on the moon.*

Apollo 11 looked like the earlier Apollo missions. The spacecraft had three parts. First was the command module, or CM. The CM was where the crew lived and from where they flew the mission. The CM looked like a cone.

The service module had equipment for keeping the crew alive and for moving the spacecraft through space. It had oxygen, water, and fuel. The lunar module detached from the rest and would land two of the crew on the moon and back to the spacecraft. The command module was called *Columbia*. The lunar module was called the *Eagle*.

NASA had been preparing for *Apollo 11* for years. After all the experiments, test flights, and fixes, it was ready to land someone on the moon.

To the Moon and Back

On July 16, 1969, a crowd gathered at the Kennedy Space Center in Florida. They were all looking at a big rocket. Atop the rocket was *Apollo 11*.

Apollo 11 lifted off at 9:32 in the morning. The crowd saw the rocket lift into the air and followed its trail of **exhaust** until it was gone from sight.

Apollo 11's flight to the moon took more than three days. Astronaut Buzz Aldrin described the days: we "just kind of gazed out the window at the Earth getting smaller and smaller, did housekeeping things, checking the spacecraft."

While flying to the moon, the astronauts talked to people on Earth through TV. They showed people what was going on.

As the astronauts got closer and closer to the moon, excitement grew. On July 20, Aldrin and Armstrong got into the lunar module. Collins stayed in the command module. They flew the lunar module down to the moon and landed successfully. Armstrong said, "The *Eagle* has landed." The lunar module had touched down in an area called the Sea of Tranquility.

For two hours, the astronauts stayed inside. They made sure everything was working right. They also ate

Exhaust is the smoke and gases left behind by a vehicle burning fuel.

Apollo 11 *was an extremely significant moment in our history—the first time a human has walked on a world other than the Earth.*

and even tried to sleep. They couldn't doze off, though. They were too excited!

Back on Earth, millions of people watched the moon landing on TV. They watched as the two astronauts opened the lunar module. They watched as Armstrong stepped out onto the moon's surface.

As Neil Armstrong first set foot on the moon, he said, "One small step for man, one giant leap for mankind." Today, that quote is famous. It means that sending humans safely to the moon was one of our biggest accomplishments as a species.

A few minutes later, Aldrin joined Armstrong outside of the module. Armstrong and Aldrin spent a couple hours exploring the moon. They tested out the best way to walk. It ended up being easier than they had thought.

While on the moon, the astronauts did a lot for science. They collected rocks. They left some experiments behind, which would send information back to Earth. They did a lot of walking, but the farthest away they got from the lunar module was only about two hundred feet.

They also stuck an American flag in the dirt. And they left a plaque nearby that said, "Here men from the planet Earth first set foot upon the Moon, July 1969, A.D. We came in peace for all mankind."

The astronauts were the first people to ever see the moon up close. Aldrin later said, "What fascinated me was the lifelessness of it. That had not changed in hundreds of thousands of years."

Although they would have liked to spend a long time exploring, they had to get back before their life support ran out. After they explored, they headed back to the lunar module. Then they slept! They hadn't had much sleep, and they had a lot of work left ahead of them.

After sleeping, the two astronauts flew back up to the command module to rejoin Collins. Then all three of the crew started the flight back to Earth.

On July 24, the command module landed in the ocean. They were picked up by the USS *Hornet*. Their journey was over. But we had just started our journeys to the moon.

A lot of what we know about the moon today came from information gathered by the astronauts of *Apollo 11*. For example, they discovered

Apollo 11's *experiments taught us much about the geology of the moon.*

TRAVELING TO THE MOON

that there was no water on the moon, and the rocks there formed *volcanically* without interacting with water. They also found that the large flat basins on the moon were caused by asteroids hitting the surface and causing flows of lava.

Apollo 11 reached President Kennedy's goal of sending someone to the moon. NASA had done it in just eight years. And the United States had won the space race.

Rocks are formed ***volcanically*** when lava cools down and hardens, Granite and basalt are examples of volcanic rock.

Find Out Even More

Reading and visiting your nearest library is one of the best ways to find more information about missions to the moon and beyond. But, remember, books can only cover so much. And no one book has all the information there is to know about a subject. Books only have so many pages. This book's author had to find information and split it up into chapters. She had to group different ideas and facts together. In this way, she's done you a big favor: you didn't have to go out and research the information yourself. But, you can never get all the information about a subject from a single book. Books are great for learning many things, but they aren't perfect.

Using the Internet is another great way to look up information about rockets leaving Earth for the moon. Unlike a book, on the Internet, there is no limit to the information you can find. You do have to search for information yourself, but there is no end to what you can learn. The Internet is one of the best ways to learn more about what you love, but it's not perfect either. Often, the best way to look for information online is by using search engines. Search engines like Google, Yahoo!, and Bing help to give you things that will be most important to you. But the sites search engines find depend on what you type into the search bar.

Search engines like Google and Bing can only find sites based on what key words you use, so picking the right words is important. Try searching for some of the words below. Type any of these subjects into the search bar on any search engine and you'll be on your way to learning even more.

Galileo
Buzz Aldrin
Apollo 1
Apollo 11
Apollo 13
Apollo 17
Neil Armstrong
Constellation program
John F. Kennedy
lunar module
National Aeronautics and Space Administration (NASA)
Sputnik

THREE

Other Notable Apollo Missions

People had reached the moon. But moon missions were far from over. Scientists knew there was a lot left to learn about the moon. So they had several more Apollo missions planned to send more explorers to the moon.

NASA sent up seven more *Apollo* missions after *Apollo 11*. Almost all of them landed people on the moon.

Apollo 12, the next moon mission, also successfully sent three astronauts to the moon. NASA just had to re-create the smooth *Apollo 11* mission again. They already knew they could do it! Now it was a matter of making sure all *procedures* and equipment were safe.

Two astronauts on *Apollo 12*—Charles Conrad Jr. and Alan Bean—walked on the moon for a total of seven hours and forty-five minutes. They collected more soil and rocks to bring back to Earth. Then they safely returned home.

A ***procedure*** is a structured way of doing things.

The crew of the USS Iwo Jima *hoists the* Apollo 13 *command module from the ocean, following its landing.*

The next mission didn't go so smoothly. *Apollo 13* has become one of the most famous moon missions in the United States. Luckily, no one was killed, but it could have been a disaster.

Apollo 13

Apollo 13 was supposed to be the third moon landing. Like the other Apollo missions, the spacecraft had three astronauts, a command module, a service module, and a lunar module. The lunar module was set to land on a crater called Fra Mauro.

NASA had originally chosen commander Jim Lovell, command module pilot Ken Mattingly, and lunar module pilot Fred Haise. Mattingly was replaced, because he had been exposed to measles. Jack Swigert took his place.

The first part of the flight went well. A few days into the mission, capsule communicator Joe Kerwin even said, "The spacecraft is in real good shape as far as we are concerned. We're bored to tears down here."

Not for long. A few hours later, something unexpected happened. The crew had just finished a TV broadcast. They showed viewers what the spacecraft was like and how they lived in space.

Just nine minutes later, the astronauts heard a loud bang, and the spacecraft shook. Swigert radioed NASA and said, "Houston, we've had a problem here."

At first, they couldn't figure out what had happened. But something had definitely gone wrong.

Warning lights showed the astronauts an oxygen tank was empty. The second one was emptying fast, too. And two of the three fuel cells were gone. Fuel cells were what gave *Apollo 13* electricity.

And to top it all off, the astronauts could see some sort of gas escaping from the spacecraft into space. It looked like an oxygen tank had exploded.

Apollo 13 the Movie

Lots of people know about Apollo 13 because of the movie by the same name. Ron Howard directed the movie in 1995. It has a lot of suspense, excitement, and drama. Howard worked with NASA to make sure the movie was accurate. Apollo 13 went on to be popular with audiences and won nine Academy Awards.

The Apollo 13 command module splashes down safely in the ocean. The astronauts inside were recovered within minutes by a helicopter sent from the U.S.S. Iwo Jima.

TRAVELING TO THE MOON

The crew of Apollo 13. *From left to right: Commander James Lovell, John Swigart, and Fred Haise.*

First, the astronauts tried to close the door between the command module and the lunar module to save oxygen. Unfortunately, it wouldn't close.

The astronauts were losing oxygen fast. They watched as the amount of oxygen in the last oxygen tank fell. If it got too low, they would run out of oxygen and die.

Together, the astronauts and NASA decided they should go into the lunar module. They could save oxygen in there. And the command module was about to lose power.

The crew of the USS Iwo Jima, *the ship that recovered the astronauts of Apollo 13, fall silent for a prayer of thanks at the astronauts' safe return.*

NASA had to figure out how to get the lunar module back to Earth. The whole spacecraft was still in one piece. Scientists could use the command and service modules to move it around. They burned up some fuel moving the spacecraft into the right position to come back to Earth.

Although *Apollo 13* didn't land on the moon, it did pass by it. *Apollo 13* circled around it and then headed back.

Now there was a new problem. The explosion had caused some pieces from the spacecraft to float off. The material in space was getting in the way of *Apollo 13*'s navigation equipment. But the astronauts had to navigate to get back to Earth. NASA came up with a way to use the sun to navigate home.

In space, the astronauts had to see if there was enough oxygen, food, and water in the lunar module to get home. They decided they did have enough oxygen. But food and water didn't look so good. The lunar module was only supposed to have enough food and water for forty-five hours. It would take them twice that long to get to Earth.

Water was the biggest problem. The astronauts needed water to drink. But the spacecraft also needed water to cool off. Without water, it could get too hot when it reentered Earth's atmosphere.

Now that everything was set with the lunar module, the astronauts just had to wait. They got closer and closer to Earth. They were tired, thirsty, cold, and scared. But they were almost home.

A few hours before landing, the lunar module detached from the rest of the spacecraft. The crew was ready to splash down into the ocean. And that's exactly what happened. They landed safely in the Pacific Ocean.

The landing was a huge relief. The astronauts had thought they might die. So did the scientists at NASA. But everyone had worked together to make sure that didn't happen.

The crew had managed to survive without a lot of food and water. By the time they got home, the three had lost almost thirty-two pounds.

NASA was shaken but still proud. It called *Apollo 13* a "successful failure." *Apollo 13* hadn't landed on the moon, but all three astronauts were home safe and sound. Even though the spacecraft had run into major problems, they had survived.

Mission controllers watch a television broadcast sent from the cabin of Apollo 13. *This mission was a failure, but fortunately all three astronauts survived.*

Apollo 17 *was the last time to date that humans have been to the moon.*

Apollo 17

After *Apollo 13*, NASA avoided more disasters. *Apollo 14, 15*, and *16* all landed on the moon safely and successfully. They all continued to give us more information about the moon. Astronauts explored new areas of the moon.

Apollo 17 was more advanced than the first Apollo missions. It had better equipment. Astronauts could spend more time on the moon. They even had a lunar roving vehicle to drive on the surface.

This mission was notable because it was the last Apollo mission. Like the other missions, astronauts gathered rocks, took photos, and did some experiments. But unlike other Apollo missions, no one was coming after this one. No humans would step on the moon to do more exploring.

The Apollo 17 *mission* included a moon rover, which the astronauts used to cover greater distances and carry more lunar samples than they normally could.

Instead, NASA moved on to other projects. It focused more on re-usable spacecraft called space shuttles. It worked on space stations, which allowed astronauts to live in space. Space was more than just the moon! It was time to learn more about the rest of the universe.

Find Out Even More

Whenever you use search engines like Google or Bing, you're going to find millions of results. Searching for "Neil Armstrong," for example, leads to millions of sites. Around 33 million if you're using Google.com!

When you search for Neil Armstrong, you'll get many different kinds of search results:

Neil Armstrong - Wikipedia, the free encyclopedia
en.wikipedia.org/wiki/Neil_Armstrong

Neil Armstrong Biography - Facts, Birthday, Life Story – Biography.com
www.biography.com › People

NASA - Biography of Neil Armstrong
www.nasa.gov/centers/glenn/about/bios/neilabio.html

DJ Neil Armstrong
www.djneilarmstrong.com

And those are just a few of the results from the first page! There are millions more, but not all search results are the same. Which of the sites above do you think would be the most useful for finding information about Neil Armstrong? Which is probably the least useful?

The official NASA site, www.nasa.gov, is probably the best result in the list of sites above. NASA.gov is a great source of information about missions to the moon and the astronauts who have walked on its surface. While DJ Neil Armstrong might be a great DJ, his site probably isn't the one we want to visit if we're looking for information about Neil Armstrong the astronaut.

Wikipedia can be a great place to get started when you want to learn a few quick facts about something you're curious about. But remember to look for the small numbers near the facts you read on Wikipedia. Clicking these numbers can lead you to the source of the information on Wikipedia. Then you can decide whether that information is useful or not. Not every fact on Wikipedia is true.

Millions of other sites have more information on Armstrong's life and moonwalk. You can never see them all, but with so much information online, you'll never run out of things to read and learn!

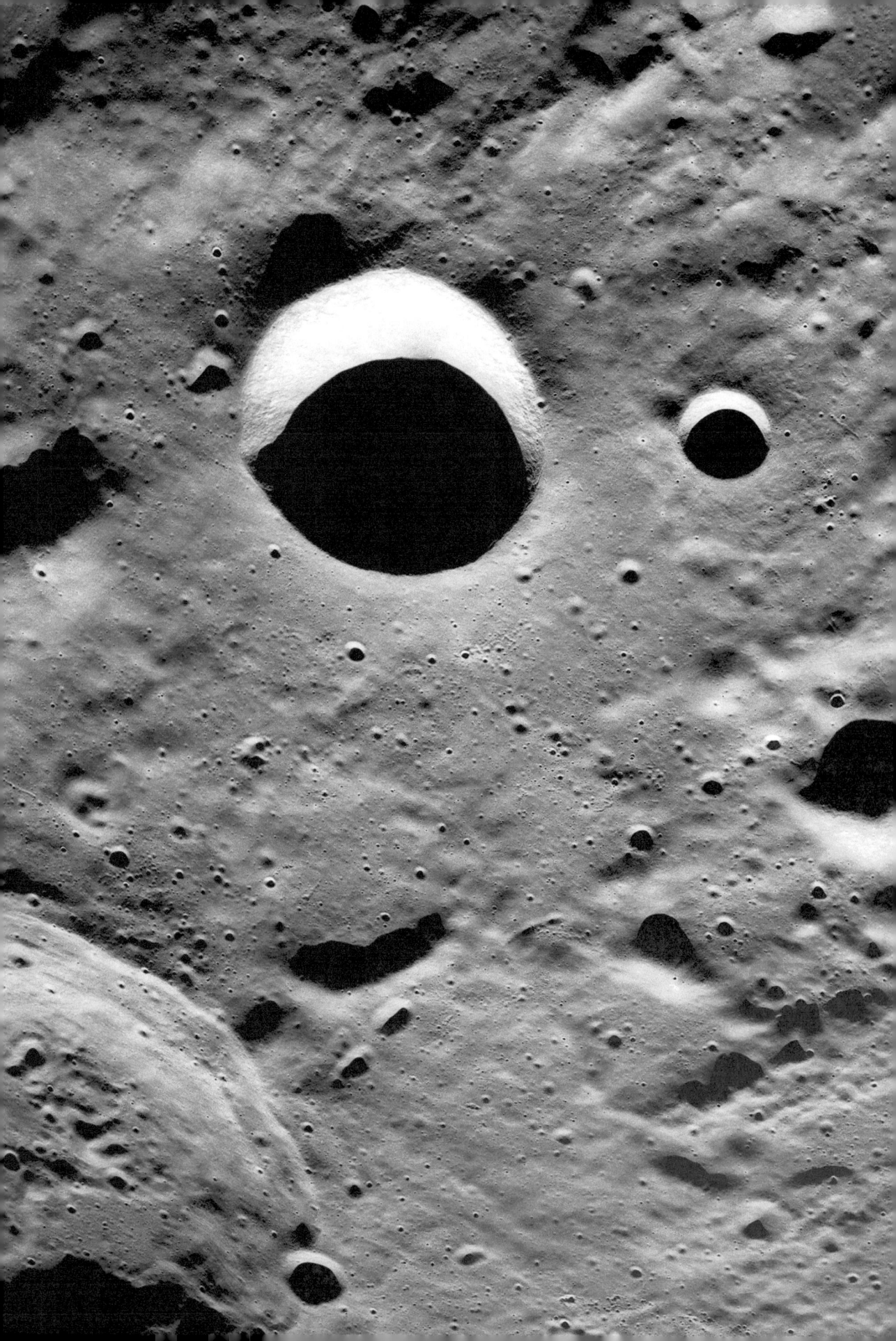

FOUR

Other Missions to the Moon

The United States and the Soviet Union (now Russia) haven't been the only countries to reach the moon. As long as a country has the right *technology*, anyone can go to the moon!

India

While the United States and Russia have mostly moved on to other space exploration projects, India has been learning a lot about the moon.

The Indian Space Research Organization (ISRO) runs the Indian space program. The ISRO came up with a moon mission program in the 2000s called Chandrayaan.

Chandrayaan-1 was a lunar orbiter that launched in 2008. It circled around the moon, looking for scientific information. It gathered data about the moon's geology. It carried equipment from India, the United States, and Europe.

> **Technology** is a tool or technique that humans invent to make a task easier.

Chandrayaan-1 was India's first lunar mission. Although the spacecraft was lost before its mission was completed, it did send back information that demonstrated that the Indian space program will continue to be useful.

The orbiter was supposed to last for two years, but it only worked for about one year. In that year, however, *Chandrayaan-1* sent back some useful information!

In 2009 the orbiter helped discover water on the moon. *Chandrayaan-1* measured lots of water molecules all over the moon's surface. Scientists think the water molecules come from the moon. Before, they thought the water came from somewhere else. Along with water, the orbiter showed that the moon had iron on its surface.

After about a year, India suddenly lost contact with *Chandrayaan-1*. But they had learned a lot of interesting things. And they weren't about to give up.

The ISRO has another Chandrayaan mission in the works. It wants to send up *Chandrayaan-2*. It would have an orbiter, along with a lander and a rover to travel the surface. If India is successful, we'll be putting human-made objects back on the moon.

China

China is another country that is looking to the moon. Right now, China has its own space lab circling Earth. It also has spacecraft. Eventually, China wants to build a space station.

China has even launched people into space. It is the third country to do so. Maybe they will eventually send someone to the moon. China has said that is one of its space exploration goals.

China's lunar exploration program is called Chang'e. The China National Space Administration (CNSA) launched the first Chang'e mission in 2007. *Chang'e 1* was a lunar orbiter, without any people onboard.

Chang'e 2 was launched in 2010. It was another unmanned orbiter. For a while, it circled the moon and collected scientific data. It took detailed photos of parts of the surface. Some of the photos might help scientists decide where to land a Chinese moon mission.

Now it's traveling into deep space—beyond the moon. In 2012 *Chang'e 2* flew by an asteroid, giving scientists close-up pictures.

Next up are more lunar missions. The CNSA hopes to land a rover on the moon and bring back rocks from the surface. And someday, Chinese astronauts may be landing on the moon.

The Future

In the United States, NASA hasn't sent anyone to the moon since *Apollo 17*. For a little while, NASA was planning on focusing on the moon again.

NASA called its program Constellation. With Constellation, NASA would send new spacecraft and more people to the moon. Under Constellation, NASA planned on building new spacecraft called Orion. It also wanted to build Ares rockets to launch the spacecraft into Earth.

The goal was to use the new spacecraft to get people to the International Space Station (the current space station, where astronauts live

The lunar module of the Apollo 14 mission. Although humans have not been to the moon since the Apollo program ended, we are continuing to make plans for future manned missions to space.

Most of NASA's rocket launches have been from the state of Florida. This view from orbit shows the bright city lights that cover the area.

and study in space). Then they would take people to the moon and maybe Mars.

However, President Barack Obama took a look at the Constellation program. The project was too big. It was too expensive. President Obama canceled the program.

NASA has new plans now. It is focusing on space station research. It's also thinking about ways to get to Mars and explore it. Space exploration won't stop!

When a mission is successful, it's very exciting! A mission like the Curiosity rover represents the hard work of thousands of people, and it's a great feeling when all that effort pays off.

The world successfully met the challenge of sending humans to the moon. Now we're looking even further. People are working hard to explore asteroids, Mars, and deep space. We can use what we've learned about traveling to the moon to someday send humans to Mars or beyond. And by exploring the moon, we've learned a lot more about our universe. There's still plenty left to discover!

Find Out Even More

Not every website is the same. Some sites have much better information than others. And with Facebook and Twitter, you need to be sure you know what you're reading and who it's coming from. Each person has a different point of view. Each of us sees the world a bit differently. It's the same online. Each site has its own point of view and its own rules about what can be posted and what cannot. A website like NASA.gov is a great source of information about the missions to the moon. A blog post by a user named IxLOVExCATS probably isn't. Remember, just because you read something on the Internet, that doesn't mean it's true.

Whenever you're reading something on the Internet or searching for information about a subject you love, ask yourself a few questions about the sites you visit:

1. Who made the site? Why did they make the site? Each website has a different point of view, so thinking about why the site was made can be a good way of deciding if the site is worth using or not.

2. Each website is different and some sites are better sources of information than others. Do you think the site you're using is a good source of information?

3. How is the site organized? Can you search for topics that you want

to learn more about? Are there categories of information to help you sort through the website?

4. Is the information you're reading on the site up-to-date or is it old? Can you find another site with more recent information? Adding "news" to the key words you're using can be a good way to find the latest facts.

5. Can you find information on this site that you couldn't find in the books you've looked through? Is there more recent information on this site than in the books you've read about the same subject?

6. What do you like about the site? Do you dislike anything about the site? Why? Would you use the site again?

Asking yourself these questions can help you pick the sites with good information from the sites that post bad information. And sorting out the two is a big part of learning about the subjects you love online. Above all, remember that there are no rules about what people can post on the Internet, and no one checks the facts on every website. Some have better information than others, and it's up to you to judge the difference.

Here's What We Recommend

If you want to to learn more about missions to the moon and space exploration, here are some good websites and books to get you started!

Online

"Discovery Kids: What Was the First Manned Moon Landing Like?" kids.discovery.com/tell-me/space/what-was-the-first-manned-moon-landing-like

Kid's Cosmos
www.kidscosmos.org/solar_system/moon_landings.php

NASA Kid's Club
www.nasa.gov/audience/forkids/kidsclub/flash/index.html

Wechoosethemoon.org
wechoosethemoon.org

In Books

Chalkin, Andrew. *Mission Control, This Is Apollo*. New York: Penguin, 2009.

Ross, Stewart. *Moon: Science, History, and Mystery*. New York: Oxford University Press, 2009.

Thimmesh, Catherine. *Team Moon: How 400,000 People Landed Apollo 11 on the Moon*. New York: Houghton Mifflin, 2006.

Woodford, Chris. *Moon Missions*. New York: Gareth Stevens Publishing, 2004.

Index

About the Author

Kim Etingoff lives in Boston, Massachusetts, spending part of her time working on farms. Kim writes educational books for young people on topics including health, science, history, and more.

Picture Credits

www.ingramcontent.com/pod-product-compliance
Lightning Source LLC
Chambersburg PA
CBHW042018080426
42735CB00002B/97